Wakefield Press

HARBOUR

Kate Llewellyn is the author of 25 books comprising poetry, memoir, travel, essays, journals, and letters. She is the co-editor of *The Penguin Book of Australian Women Poets*. Her book *The Waterlily: A Blue Mountain Journal* sold over 35,000 copies and is soon to be republished. Kate was the first National Secretary of the Poets Union of Australia and now lives in Hove, South Australia.

T0363965

Also by Kate Llewellyn

Novels
Dear You (1988)

Journals
The Waterlily (1987)
The Mountain (1989)
Burning (1997)
Playing With Water (2005)
A Fig at the Gate (2014)

Letters
First Things First: Selected Letters of Kate Llewellyn 1977–2004 (2015)

Autobiography
The Dressmaker's Daughter (2008)

Travel
Angels and Dark Madonnas: Travels in India and Italy (1991)
Lilies, Feathers & Frangipani (1993)
Gorillas, Tea and Coffee: An African sketchbook (1996)

Poetry
Trader Kate and the Elephants (1982)
Luxury (1985)
Honey (1988)
Figs (1990)
Selected Poems (1992)
Crosshatched (1994)
Sofala and Other Poems (1999)

Essays
The Floral Mother and Other Essays (1995)

Edited
The Penguin Book of Australian Women Poets (1986)
with Susan Hampton

HARBOUR

Poems 2000–2019

Kate Llewellyn

**Wakefield
Press**

The author and publisher thank the editors and publishers of the following publications and anthologies in which some of these poems first appeared: *The Australian Book Review*, *The Best Australian Poems of 2004 and 2005*, edited by Les Murray, Black Inc., and *The Best Australian Poems 2006*, edited by Judith Beveridge, University of Queensland Press. Also the *Canberra Times* and *Weekend Australian*, *Heat*, *Island*, *Kunappi*, *Meanjin*, *Overland*, *Quadrant* and *Southerly*.

Wakefield Press
16 Rose Street
Mile End
South Australia 5031
www.wakefieldpress.com.au

First published 2020

Cover designed by Liz Nicholson, Wakefield Press
Edited by Julia Beaven, Wakefield Press
Text designed and typeset by Michael Deves, Wakefield Press

ISBN 978 1 74305 702 5

NATIONAL LIBRARY OF AUSTRALIA

A catalogue record for this book is available from the National Library of Australia

CORIOLE
McLAREN VALE

Wakefield Press thanks Coriole Vineyards for continued support

CONTENTS

HARBOUR

When I first sailed into Sydney Harbour
I cried. A man standing, watching,
asked what was up.
'It's so beautiful,' I said
and he replied, 'Oh to be so young.'

Now old, beauty no longer makes me cry.
Instead, from time to time, there are
glimpses of what else matters
and a chance to act.
While I can't erase what I did
there is the gift, the opportunity,
knowing that time is short
the little casual things
I didn't see turned into a roar
I no longer can ignore.

It is this, the chance of grace
that consoles my slowing pace.

OXYTOCIN

On this bright morning
a cruel wind is up.
I don't care –
last night I strode among the stars.
Black swan shelter in the sandhills' lee,
while pelicans stand preening
on the lagoon's edge.
We each must share our little pill
of poison – a tattooed drummer,
a drunk, a married man –
while we sit at kitchen tables
drinking tea with other women.
Rain pelts down the windows
while we talk about the promises
they made. It's enough to make
you laugh since it's only down
to chemicals. When oxytocin floods
the brain, fools and dills
and maniacs look irresistible.
I don't care –
last night I strode among the stars
and my brain drank by the gallon
the chemical that makes me think
he's wonderful.
Now I'll need a thousand cups of tea
and tears measured by the litre

to flush the oxytocin from my brain.
Sunsets seem meaningful,
rain is glistening on the neighbour's roof
like tears. The rhapsody of nature
only underwrites that last night
I strode among the stars.

DAWN

The morning star rises
and below, is a plane coming in
like a butterfly with a torch.

Across the train line,
a light appears
somebody has put on the kettle.

Trees are black shapes
crouching, hiding the secrets of the day.
The radio continues, as it has all night
providing dreams or news
which I share with old single people
who have developed this habit.

A train passes lit
like a fallen Christmas tree
and the day, rested, stretches
and begins.

Children
shrug on their bags.
Thousands of coffee machines
heat up, while dogs wag their tails
and let their tongues hang out
waiting to walk.
The smell of toast announces
the rising of the phallus
at this inconvenient hour.

THE BIG NOTHING

(For Ian North)

He arrives 27 hours late
but always welcome.
'Can we walk away from the light?'
he says. So we head off,
our backs to the sea –
(I'd thought sunsets and reflections
were what he'd be after).

Walking slowly on beside the railway line
he stops, raises his old Hasselblad
and says, 'Can you stand behind?'
(Shadows interfere.) A car comes.
'Blast,' he says and waits.

What is it that he sees?
Trees, a Stobie pole –
the way light falls –
it looks like nothing much to me.
Emptiness really,
the abyss that light leads to,
it sets my teeth on edge.

He takes the picture
and on we go. Again, a stop.
A bike interrupts this time then a car.
The light is changing,
more of big fat nothing

that only he can see while I stand
holding my shadow in my hand
Thrice more we halt
and then we shuffle home well pleased.

Art is always like this
mysterious as light.

DIRT

Then, just when I thought
for me it was all over,
I fell in love with dirt.
Mr Right at last.
Wife of Dirt.
I slaved over him
and was ravished,
year in year out. Not just in spring
and summer when he can escape
his wife, but other seasons too.
Camellias are our winter quilt
and in autumn, I know he's true
when his face is striped in shadows
of the trees.
At last, a faithful lover
solemn, silent, magisterial,
profound and mysterious –
all the things I like in a man.
I've always been a bolter
but this time
I'll go to my grave with him.

BROTH

Sometimes, when I've got poems
pasted all over me like wet confetti
and not one will come off, I make broth.

Bone broth, chicken broth,
or, when in a hurry, Bovril.
You see, I must save my strength –

Even the new neighbours,
seeing my situation, often left broth in a jar
on the step
which I drank feebly
with gratitude.
But still the poems would not come off
and then I gave up.

Gardening daily, more interested
in the snouts of tulips breaking the soil
than this old wet confetti
which, with a will of its own,
peels from my face, hair and limbs
falling onto these snowy pages
like rain
onto the snouts of the tulips.

THE JUG

Beautiful, new and as perfect
as hands and nature could make it.
I had the jug for a couple of years
in all its perfection.

The jug was heaven on earth –
full of love and kindness
which fell from its lip
blessing my life with grace.

I smiled every time
I saw the jug and couldn't believe
my fortune. Of course,
beauty such as this is desirable,
highly so.

From the time the boy saw the jug
he was filled with desire.
With desire comes envy.
He took the jug, spat into it
and handed it back.

FROST

Three frosts in a row
all welcome for sweetening
the blood oranges.
Also, somehow making me cheerful.
We all need something
to push against.

Eve showed that,
when fed up with Adam, no work
and eternal bliss,
she took her chance.

I leap up, take the engineless mower
and rush at the sea of grass like a racing yacht
among the waves of frost leaving a green wake
steered by my hands
once like lilies,
now mallee roots.

THE TENT

The tent is finally pitched –
tight and secure
all pegs deeply embedded.

Inside, the air mattress lies, fully pumped
plump as a peach.

But something's awry –
the tent needs to be moved –
over there where it will be cooler
at noon.

After hours of slog, it's done.
Taught and smart, the tent is erected
it's perfect.
But it is under a gum tree
and we all know what can happen
in the night under a gum.
It won't do.
The tent must be moved.
It's a matter of safety –
utterly crucial.

'I don't care how weary you are,
just come and give me a hand.'
The tent, let down, subsides
to the earth and is dragged
along to a better site.

Here it stands,
erect and beautiful as a phallus.

But there's something wrong –
hard to put your finger on it
it's just not right –
let me think about it.

THE ENGLISH TRADITION

Grace will do all it can
to describe his isolation
sitting in the garden drinking tea
longing to hear the birds.

He can remember the sea
through a port-hole
and later watching a painting fade
at the end of his bed.

Clouds pass above
as we walk.
I don't mention them
because who can describe a cloud,
needing first to mention sky?

In the coracle of our friendship
shaped like a sickle moon
all that is left to say
is he has passed through my life
like the wind in the trees.

THE JETTY

We step onto the old wooden finger
and walk into the sunset
talking and pointing.
We've not lost poetry
although one of us thinks she has.
No, it was crouching there
like this fisherman loading his hook
as we pause to look
into his bucket which is not exactly empty
but full of hope.
On the horizon, the line of pink
is audacious,
stern in fact, not sentimental
as pink can often be,
more like a line of prophecy
ripped from an old book.
At the end, we peer into the water
looking for life, or anything at all,
turn, link arms, stroll back
spread a white cloth on a table,
and then, while we drink tea,
one reads her poems to the other
who, as if she is catching measles,
becomes infected after all these years.

SPREAD

Fences and roads are no good
to us – we must spread.
Whatever the size, it's not enough.
We seep like water around buildings,
over roads, out the door,
into the garden, down to the beach –
into the sea.

We take a swag, or a spade a ute
a dog and a gun. Or simply a barrow
or nothing at all. Then we just start
weeding.
Pull the first weed, you'll take a second,
In a month, you'll have a garden.
In a year, you'll have spread.
You'll have a farm, then a station.

People will help you.
They'll see you bent over
and they'll wind down the window
and ask what you are doing.
'As you see, I'm making a garden.'
'Do you want some plants?'

Strength leads strength to strength
and spread leads spread to spread.
Nuns and monks chant all night
and nuns and monks chant all day
then spread is called faith.

TUCKER

Even as a child
his black eyes would pierce you
like a stick.
I'm still, like many others,
afraid of him —
his bulls and cows and sheep,
his rutting deer in the night.

This is my year of healing
and one of the worst explosions
of my life came from a stranger
and half killed me.

Yet, consolingly, my brother makes
small gracious speeches
when he rings daily at dusk
on his latest project.

We are both grateful
I can be of help to him.
Before, perhaps, only a nuisance.

I think of the great skies
floating above his land –
and when I walk down his drive
of dark pine trees to his home
black cockatoos scream and rise
like calligraphy on the sky from a sibyl
unfathomable as who will die first.

The infinity of land and sky
and work,
his endurance and nobility
are measured by our silence
and the screaming cockatoos.

WHAT I HAVE LOST

Great-grandfather's stamp collection
A gold sovereign
My mother's silver bracelet (in a sand dune)
Friends
Watches galore
Some hearing
Opportunities
A brace of lovers
Several stone
Parents
A dinner set (at Central Station)
A husband
Luggage
Recipes
My father's moth-eaten maroon woollen bathers
Teeth
Desire for revenge.

THE DAY

Under its grey hat
of sky
a scarf of clouds
the day departs the dawn
and firmly shuts the door.

Busily it passes
with white egret stalking.
The day has purpose
it does not stop to stare.
It has a lot to get through:
lunch, dinner, rose-planting
and other priorities.
A million factories to start
and stop
schools, offices, road works
and other mighty operations,
Oh busy happy
beautiful day.
How many are there
of you left?

MORNING

The yellow chair and the red
sit at the pine table on the verandah
waiting for tea.

The voice of that crow
I can't kill
saws through the chairs' legs.

Green hills sit hands in laps
smoke coming from their nostrils.
Here come the guinea fowl
last to roost and first to rise –
a flock of nuns ringing their tiny bells.

An island floats in the dam
a burnt meringue in a green jelly.
One wild duck drags its silver victory flag
around and around the dam
while the blond boy sleeps on
in this old wooden house
sailing through the breathless morning.

THE BOAT

All day I row a dinghy
and at night rest the oars
within their rowlocks
yet I move increasingly asleep
or wide awake towards the vast horizon
lit by stars.

New Zealand looms
and islands pass while I plough
the paddocks of the sea.
This wooden boat cannot last
none ever do –
packed with house and garden,
dolls and pens and clothes and books.

Now I see that all my life
I've taken shortcuts –
I garden with a knife –
but the Pacific Ocean offers
no quick way.

My tangles of concern
are nets not meant for me.
What I must do is row
and rest and marvel at the stars
until I feel a bump
then the boat becomes a coffin
made of leaves.

WELCOME

Brigid Rose, you have come to live
among us
and we are over the moon.
Although you have come too soon,
and can't drink yet, love
and milk are introduced to you
giving you all you need.

Brigid Rose, you are performing
miracles on us all including your
father,
who, his father says,
'... is a changed man. He loves her.'
Well, I admit, he was a loving man before,
but
with you he is different.

Brigid Rose, while you lie there
sleeping, thinking things over or dreaming
remembering the drum of your mother's heart,
we are joyful. You have come to us
from infinity, you were once stardust
and now you are you.
The nurses
touch you gently, and speak softly
while we wait and watch
gratefully.

For, from the time you took
your first breath, you gave
us life because in your living
we all live more.

THE DRESSMAKER'S DAUGHTER

I was the dressmaker's daughter
our dialogue was fabric, colour
embroidery, pins and scissors.
The almost silent sound
of snipped cloth falling
on the table round my feet.

A bodice of pins drawn down
over my head like a scaffold.
I spent my childhood in the sea
or standing on a table –
'A sway back!' she said proudly.
Once I wore a tablecloth as a skirt
to school and before that curtains
as a dress.
I was always proud. The colours
clung like flowers. I was summer,
autumn spring. Never winter.
'See,' she'd say, 'a pocket.'
cutting fabric to a map like Australia
then inserting flagpoles of pins
on the beaches.
'You can never match blue!'
Bodice, baste, peplum, flare,
dart, placket, gusset, yoke.
Air suddenly swept round my legs
then my armpits grew cool

as the cold blades clipped
and my shoulder appeared.
There are no scars as no flesh
was ever snicked so nothing bled.
No sister interrupted
the lavish pageant
the geometry of adornment.

THE BRIDESMAID

Hello, here you are again
haunting and sulking
just because you didn't catch my flowers.
I can see this is going to go on and on –
talk about 'til death us do part'!

Arriving yesterday in Woolworths
was pretty low – I had to take
those buffers from the shelves
paracetamol swallowed dry
and Dencorub applied
beneath my jacket's collar.
Even so you clung on
nagging and whining
until I escaped you on the bike
but then you got your own back
in the night.
I tossed and turned while you gloated.
Why can't we be friends?
Call a truce – or are you one of those,
who, losing one enemy
must right away make another?

TEN

The high dome of nought
towers beside the lone poplar of one.
Two, questions their addition
and trails off with an uncertain sigh.
Three holds hands with itself
and laughs with delight
thinking how clever and lucky it is.
Four knows what it is to be out
of fashion eternally square
and is resigned.
Five is confused and despairing
as it began going backwards,
lowered itself, then hastily managed
a forward thrust and fell to backwardness
again.
Six, seeing this, became determined
so made a simple statement –
a tree by a pond,
and left it at that.
Seven was quick, it drew the horizon
and a well and let the philosophers
consider its meaning.
Eight smiled and sat on itself
content as two men in love.
Nine ended it all,
managing the moon and a fall

some would say there's a lesson there.
Ten needs a marriage before it can breed
and invent a bible of numbers
while history waits
longing to read
before the large dome of nought
swallows it all.

TELEPHONE

You ought to ring up.
The farm may have disappeared
into the river – as it does from time to time –
or the trees in the orchard bloomed with stars
or the geese may have rowed
in the blue dinghy adorned with hundreds
of marigolds to the island
with six of them sitting straight up
on the bench, the other two heaving an oar
while the rooster watches appalled
on the shore.
The peacocks may have grown tails
orchestrated with shimmering eyes
and breasts of celestial blue.
One may have turned white
overnight and resemble nothing more
than a bride who fled afraid
to a branch of the old mango tree
where she stays sullen and stubborn
refusing our blandishments to afternoon tea.
For all you know, the sky at dusk
may have entered the river
and bled there giving birth to the night.
The bauhinia tree may have turned pink
and filled itself up with small birds
trembling like thumbs given wings.
Oh, at last the phone rings.

SLEEP

1.

To enter the bed we kneel
and fall into the white abyss.
Sleep is a form of fainting.
The altar of the pillow swirls with wisps
Of fading consciousness – a priest
comes down the aisle flicking dreams out
from an ancient ewer.

2.

Watch a sleeping man
even then they still seem astonishing
to me with an air of tragedy
like a fallen horse.
His conversation with the night
is not the same as mine,
our personalities are the sheets
on which we sleep
and no amount of washing
wears them out.

3.

Soft snores from sleeping children
the flicker of a limb –
their depth of sleep – entranced, they seem
to travel sucking their thumbs
in the carriage of their cot
across the ruts of history.

4.
A ward of sleeping women
is a peaceful boat
jaws unleashed like brassieres,
they lie trusting on the deck.
Their devoted illnesses sleep beside them
only the doctors' notes clipped like love letters
to the bed
reveal the destination of each affair.

CLEOPATRA'S EXHALATION

Who am I?
I am the light that wakes you
the baby's wet and shining gums
and its bath water
which your mother washed her face in
and the impulse that made her do it
to prolong her beauty.

I am the sparkling waves
which the blind man cannot see
and his memory of ocean
once seen through a porthole.

I am the soft foot of a child
the grunt and moan of love
and birth. The starch and whiteness
of a choirboy's robe
the voice that rises through the nave.

The bird splashing,
the frog calling in the night
and the stars reflected in the pond.
The fog that falls and rises
as an exhalation Cleopatra once made.
The knowledge that beauty comes on
endlessly
the wind moving over grasses.
Nations rise and fall
but I go on forever.

Remember I was there laying out the earth
and the endless rise and fall of tide.
I am always present
and hold you in my hand
tenderly as a pulsing frog.

THE VISITOR

Hello my lovely!
with your blouse and wide apart eyes.
Every night you talk to me
nodding and smiling.
I sit here in bed smiling back at you.
You might be a nurse or Matron herself
pausing to chat on her round,
or my daughter visiting.
Like the Queen you are unavailable
and that is how it should be.
I have no wish to show you
the garden, drink tea with you
or to hold your baby.
Serene and ethereal
you are reliable
close, yet distant
like a common angel
one flick and you're off
the square screen
keeps our friendship green.

SUMMER III

In the sultry calm
of a summer's day
the koel bird was calling.
The mournful song rang out at dawn
and at intervals all day
interspersed by crows.
The surface of the frog pond trembled
and at one end a froth of spawn
lay behind a lily.
An idea of a palm tree lay
sketched against the sky
by one who left the work abandoned.
The first gardenias appeared
and swirled their scent around.
While grevillea arched the drive
and fed the lorikeets.

Summer's silence stretched the day
as if the earth was yawning.
A crack of thunder split the air
as hour by hour stalked past
while she lay on the couch and wondered
what should I be doing?
Could breathing be a form of prayer?

THE SEA

(for Ian North and Mirna Heruc)

Side by side
they walked into the room.
Their friends parted like the sea.
The two stood there
and the bride gave herself away
a shell on a beach.
They made promises.
I admit there were many marriages
that day in that place
but like our birth and our death
each one is unique
splendid and rare
a blue parrot in Antarctica.
Later her small beaded bag
was lying on a chair.
It was the colours of the sea
with a wave of tassels
that caught the light.
All night it lay there
poignant as a shoe found
at an accident.
It seemed not unlike the bride
full of quiet qualities
often overlooked
but once seen
stay in the mind
gleaming like the sea.

PICKING ARUM LILIES

Although they are nothing in themselves
but the flesh of plants
they seem full of meaning
as I cut them damp with dew
white and scentless,
their dark plates of leaves
sprinkled with petals of the may.

They are thought by some
to be unlucky or funereal.
They are though my reward
from the barrowloads in mud
I dug out from the creek.
Inspired and sweating
sometimes I rested by the barrow
in the gutter then trailed the load
across the railway line.
The blooms lolled white with yellow tongues
as if fainting and foretelling
the exact spot one month later
that the girl would step out
into the express
which dug her like a lily
from the straight iron creek.

SEEDS

The pomegranate seeds have worked.
You fed her those at dinner
in that old pink hotel by the lake
like a farmer feeding Ratsak
mixed with liver to a crow.
But you have reckoned without me.
You've announced in numerous legends
you'll not be leaving your wife
I hope to God you don't –
ruin three lives, not four.
I know you're smitten,
you only use seeds
when you've spotted something
you want and know you can't
otherwise have – and is half the age
that you are. Yes, I admit
she's enjoying the darkness
down there in your lair of secrets,
dead birds and bones.
But she's a creature of light,
of the sun, beaches.
Your cold gloomy pool lit with forty-
watt globes
won't satisfy her in the long run.
She'll want to come up to the light.
I know you don't care

how much you've cost
and what you have ruined and smashed.
But read *Birthday Letters* and think.
Do us all a favour, let her go,
go hunting.
Shoot a crow
kill a stag
be a man
give her the antidote –
it's not too late
although there's a chill in the air.

SHADOWS

Shadows are like India –
the richness, underlining every colour –
the camels, elephants and cows
that stroll our streets and lie beneath
the trees. Saris draped to dry
on fences and small bushes.
Carts of hay drawn by bullocks
with women holding babies trailing
their legs like shadows over the blazing road.
Clouds like the Taj Mahal traverse the sea
shoals of fish and pods of whales
shelter in the shade. An ageless architecture
free for all to gaze on even here.

Show a baby if you will, your hand's shadow
on the wall. It could be a bride's hennaed hand
adjusting the jewels around her neck.
Then say the word 'shadow'.
To India you can take him later.

THE SEARCH

Where did you find it?
I can't remember exactly where
but there was light and water,
a steady rhythm –
a butcher bird was calling
then a magpie answered
crows beat on and on.
I keep searching trying to remember
but it eludes me. It's always ephemeral
you see, so almost impossible
to grasp and yet, some people
have it and seem to never lose it.
Sentimentality, I know, drives it off –
so who, I ask, is never sentimental?
Rather few, and I'm not one of them.
That stern ardour
we all long for
serves as the cord of a dressing gown
you could hang yourself with it
or lasso the numinous – it's up to you
go and look behind the door.

HEN

I am the dreaming hen
at dusk I do not glance
at the red sky staining the river.
I know much more than this awaits me
as I leap into the darkness of the curry tree.
With my head tucked under my wing
I proceed to traverse the sky.
The rooster's inflamed implacable eye
appears as a lake stained with sky
and his red rustling feathers
are storm warnings
to the meteorologist in the south.
The crow who eats my eggs
appears as a chemist
for whom I develop indecent longings.
Distressed, I consult my avian address book
searching for the place of better dreams –
something involving peaches
dropping in the orchard.
Just after dawn when it is coldest
there's a shuffling in the hen house
inside my curry tree
where the others roost.
The day rises like a hero
to the rooster's cry.

THE LODGER

Sometimes at night I smell toast
and I know the old priest
is making breakfast.
He thinks I don't know he lives here
rising when I sleep, a shadow
shuffling round the kitchen
with the lights off.
From time to time a whiff from a cigarette
rises from beneath my room.
I imagine him down there crouched
on the old mattress.

He is my better half
the faith I fail in.
The discipline and modesty
of quiet rituals. His old black cassock
hangs on a hook behind the wardrobe door:
he thinks it's hidden there.
His beret lies like a cat on the pantry shelf.
I ignore it. Why did he come?
When will he go? This sweet enigma
undemanding, shuffling through the house
with the faith of our fathers
his breath like violets.

BICYCLING

Bicycling is like philosophy
a balanced moving with invisible support
depending on a circularity that carries nonetheless
a forward motion which the moment that it stops
Causes a complete collapse.

The airy going forward uses blood
pumped energetically with argument or journey
going to new realms of thought or to the beach
or shops or simply up a hill.

The feeling of the wind
the effort so exhilarating with the view
that changes as the thing progresses.

The pounding of the sea
the mounting bricks of logic
the rhythm of the heart –
enjoyment and delight
which can be an obsession
that seems harmless early on
but reaching greater realms, can lead to nightmares
fit for Nazis, drugs, strokes and heart failure.

And yet both are also occupations for the gentle
for the dreamer, with a certain elegance
limitless to age or the need for humour.

Although a bike's a funny thing
unlikely as a platypus
and so is a philosopher
sitting at a table changing the world
and history just by thinking.

THE GENERAL

Her life's a battlefield
bodies lie around her but she's erect
giving commands to the grass and trees.

The officers died first and other generals next.
Now a few locals and other ranks –
who she overlooked, appear
from time to time on the horizon
where dusk is staining the clouds.
Sometimes they bring her sustenance
but it's dangerous work
she's still got ammunition
and her gun's well greased
with ire and discipline.

Nobody's happy,
the locals don't like it –
they must bury the dead.
Bereft and amazed she stands
her ground courageously
counting her bullets
seething with plans.

THE LIVING ROOM

It was where they sat at night
beside the fire
or with the windows open
for the soft sea breeze.
The radio and conversation
the click of knitting needles
the tap tap of his pipe
as he cleared the ash.
In the morning something
lay there extended by the night
a dress smocked like the sea
a jumper cardigan or little coat
beside the ashes of his pipe.
Their talk joined all that other
married talk
a man and a woman
speaking of a life in love.
Every Saturday I entered,
closed the door, switched on the radio
and spent three hours at work.
I ran the carpet sweeper back and forth,
then with a broken comb tidied up the carpet's fringe.
I was in another world
taking ornaments form every shelf
gently dusting them.
The handmaiden of the marriage.

Sanctity and happiness were mine
as the kero duster moved across the table.
Sometimes I danced enchanted
in that dark and gloomy room
the exalted palace of a marriage.
At noon I emerged restored and purified
almost holy.

DAWN (2)

Blinking and sighing
dawn thinks 'Oh not again'
and lifts its nightdress to the day.
The creek, sensing this
blushes, turns with the tide
and mullet begin to jump
showing their white bellies
to the camphor laurels.
The white peacock flexes
in the mango tree
and leaps like a bridesmaid.
Crows, the day's fleas, begin to bite.
Sky removes its pink feathered hat
and shoves on something practical.
A peacock begins to howl
the day is born
with cries, curses and acclamations
while work puts on its boots.

THE SONG

I dreamt I held a jar
and into it the singer's song
was poured.
Again the singer sang
and I despaired
the jar was full of song
I couldn't gather more.
Sacrificing, as we must,
I poured the song
into the ground
that I may take in more.
All night I poured and gathered
the invisibility of art
and at dawn the glass was empty
yet I rose restored.

RICE

The crust of bread
the grain of rice
a chickpea on the floor
a bean sprout in the sink.
These things seem significant –
the wasted life.

The accident, a glance away,
a moment, a blink
or years of chasing rubbish
searching for the high-pitched moment.

How everyone wants life.
The compost heap seething
in the shade. Outside this window
bright orange cumquats
packed with seed
sucking up the sun.

Once I roasted the warm wild duck
which a car hit on the road.
When rice grains fall
tormented, I glean
them from the floor.

Then I think of sperm
and am defeated.
Here, old men in frocks
take over.

POSSIBLY

How's Possibly doing today?
She's O.K. she's possibly
recovering from a possible asthma attack.
What's Possibly doing? The impossible,
that's what. Attending to twenty students
some of whom will possibly fail
tasks Possibly set which they feel
are impossibly high.
Possibly is cooking dinner for ten
and being polite in impossibly demanding
situations. Possibly would like to take a break
from her situation but can't possibly
because she needs the money.

Her impossible husband
will possibly rock up for Christmas
needing money and certain other things.
Possibly talks to me
about Milton and Sophocles.
She brings in the washing laughing
knowing she'll possibly manage
and between the cracks of impossible demands
find happiness sometimes sitting
at our picnics drawing the headland
which resembles an ancient Roman.

LOAVES AND CURRANT BUNS

Here they are
please accept my latest.

Bestirred by Jelena,
hearing her read her new poems
at dusk by the sea
as we drank tea
sitting at the table with the cloth.
Two elderly men came up to ask
what we were doing
(and 'Why is she so beautiful?'
was under their breath).

As I sat listening, something stirred
and it was not just sugar in the tea.
I thought I can do that.
As one day a child skips in the yard
at lunchtime
and later, at recess,
every small girl is skipping.
Or, as a woman feels the first kick
of her foetus.

I felt poetry rise
as a baker, touching the dough at dawn
knows it is ready and the oven hot.

Here are my loaves
and here are my currant buns.

MEMORY

My life is a mystery to me.
Only with fifty-three years of the diary
could I decipher what happened
and where I was
and how I got there.

Where were my children
when he said, 'Go away to the clouds.'
Where was my husband?
Had he left?

I've no idea.
I can tell you
when I learnt to grow tulips –
two yeas ago.
And when I got rid of the lawn –
four years ago, or perhaps three.

Yet of when I bought this house
all I can say is that it was early
this century.

What Akmatova calls
'The high freedom of the soul'
allows me to forget,
while I bury the compost
under the vine leaves stacked

like pages above the potato plants,
and then, straightening up,
watch the sparrows embroidering the garden
with their ecstatic flight.

WHAT THEY SAID

Galway Kinnell said, in a bar, late at night, 'You've got charisma.'

Mother said, 'As sure as God made apples, you'll come a cropper my girl.'

The youngest brother said, 'I'm the most successful one in our family.'

Mother said, 'I'd like to come back as a sparrow.'

Father said, 'There was a little girl, who had a little curl …'

Granny said, 'Tommy, that girl's got asthma.'

The American said, 'I am not sure if I can live without the masterpiece that is your back.'

Mother said, 'One girl is more trouble than three boys put together.'

The poet said, 'Good on you, love. The whole Department's being trying for years to get in to the *Australian*.'

Father said, 'All things in moderation.'

Granny said, 'The big winds come when the pear tree is in blossom.'

The teacher said to my mother, when her brother was fighting for Australia in Flanders, 'You funny, clumsy little German girl.'

Father said, 'Where's your straw, Jill?' So I'd put my little hand on my head.

When I turned eighty, the hairdresser said, 'Can you get to the bathroom on your own?'

Some people say as I mount my bike, 'You're not going to ride that, are you?'

Mother said, 'Don't go to Maslin Beach.'

The patient said, when his soiled dressing gown which I'd washed, was stolen, 'Now you'll have to buy me a new one.'

Mother said, 'You already know how to cook and clean, so now you must go to the apron factory and learn how to sew and then you'll be ready to marry.'

The pen said, 'I like to write quite nicely, but the owner doesn't try.'

Her mother said, 'I don't crochet. I knit. Nana crochets.'

Mother said, 'You children don't know how lucky you are. Your father never stays at the bar; he just has one beer and comes home.'

Mother said, lashing on her green apron, when she heard a child had drowned in a dam, or a farmer had died when his tractor rolled on him, 'I'll make that woman some shortbread.'

Ian said, as he sat in a dry creek bed drawing a tree, 'Draw it the way it grows.'

Father said, of my best friend's educated parents, 'They're clever lunatics.'

Mother said, 'It's all come true. Dad said – don't you remember? – "One day he'll throw you away like this old slipper!"'

THE MARRIAGE (2)

Before he left
he sat in his chair
his back towards me.

I lay on the lawn
under the Hills hoist
and gave birth to the death
of our marriage.

There was no midwife
only Dr Grief and he,
knowing the howling
must finally cease,
stood quietly by
neither holding my hand,
as the anaesthetist had
during the birth of our son,
nor offering pethedine or gas.

His profession, on this occasion
was to witness
and witness he did.
I rolled on the ground
and hugged my belly
the sorrow coming in waves.

I hadn't the wit to time it
nor did the doctor, but he knew

it would cease only when it stopped.
There was plenty of time.

The three of us there,
he, the doctor and me
and the death of our marriage
emerged groan by awful groan.

He sat still as a stone
and the hoist hung
like a gallows above me
still bellowing like a cow in heat
on the lawn.

Until, slowing, silence fell
and I stood. Empty and hollow
knowing it was done.

There are those who say that it was I
who left him.
They were not there.

THE PACT

(for Ian North)

We forget how many years
we've kept the pact
Mrs I Beg Your Pardon
and Mr Whisper.
I press the phone to my ear
and say my name. Again, he whispers
his opinion, which I value highly.

For decades most Thursdays at 4 pm
you will find us being faithful
to the pact. He tells me what he has done
I tell him what I have.
Now I realise I've learnt much
this way, including the fact
that it's possible to write a poem
in the ten minutes before 4 o'clock.

He tells me if and where
he's been working with his Hasselblad.
What clouds obliged, or roads he saw
packed full of nothing valuable
that I can see, which is the secret
of his art.

I read him the latest
and he whispers a question
or a comment.

Never underestimate the rarity
of intelligence. I state my name,
(but not my rank) for the pleasure
of hearing this again.

We're like old soldiers
addicted to marching
upright but shaky, so far
undefeated.

THE PERSIAN GARDEN

I can't go to the Persian gardens with you.
Even years ago it wouldn't have been possible –
we did though visit some gardens of the Moguls.

And now lying under these stars listening to jazz
because there are no carpets left
and these stairs are rough
you've given me your jacket to rest on.

Here is our bed
the only one we will have now.
The shape of the mosque is etched
in pink against the sky.

Our bodies side by side
like notes of music falling
from that trumpet
and the drum beats on.

The warm night air is our sheet.
This is where our lives meet
on these ancient stairs
surrounded by dark gardens.

ORDINARY SUBLIME

We will all miss it
the heavenly house and its garden into which she's put her all.
The ease and grace. She gave it to us
abundantly as stars. Nursing me upstairs
while I lay coughing looking at William Robertson's
search for the numinous in landscape.

The gleaming horse skin screen
lighting up a dark corner of the living room
I didn't see until she pointed to it
and so much else it took me years to notice.

She gave us hospitality as abundantly
as stars. Their four girls grew up here
fighting and baking.
Then one came down the stairs a bride.
Father now frail, wishes he had died
earlier. (The house is up for sale.)

And as age wrinkles all of us
like those gold and silver papers
around the boxes by the tree – the last one
here for them.

Whatever we love
we must leave. But like a book
it exists in our imagination.
A great-grandchild has come

and she can clap her hands
and make another home –
all it takes is love and a million hours
of work in a search
for the ordinary sublime.

CHRISTMAS POEM (3)

I always took a house
full of sleeping children as a normal thing
until they sent their own back.

The post girl on her motorbike has stuck
antlers on her helmet
which in the wind flatten eastwards.
In a world of kitsch even cute
can seem significant.

At dawn a strange bird was calling
like a sobbing dog. Then magpies
took over gargling the morning star
and still the children slept.

Last night's rain has pooled
in the gazebo's roof and makes it sag.
Gardenias, oriental liliums and a dragonfly
mean that it is Christmas.
Towels dry on the railing
and every afternoon it rains.
Leaves hold drops of water
each one a ball of light.

Year after year the search for faith
goes on. My heels are spurred with ardour.
Old texts seem more precious in December
and stars and sleeping children full of meaning.

CHRISTMAS POEM (6)

Overnight it rained.
The blue hydrangeas take it
as birds drink from their parents.

It's always like this, sudden changes
even in drought – as the angel gave Mary
the shock of that lily. And I tell people
the story when they stop at the gate
and ask the name of the lily.
It's news to them and they pass on
puzzled or glad I can't tell.
(I hear there's a new interest in these tales
that mainly only the elderly know.)

The post-girl chugs past on her bike
wearing a Santa Claus hat – giving always goes on
so she's frantic.
Love has never been lost
it just got confused. The physics of faith
pealed out in those carols the choir sang
last week at dusk as Diana and I rose to our feet
to sing with the people
'Hark! The Herald Angels Sing'.
And here the rain is still pouring down
filling the buckets
I eagerly placed on the lawn.

CHRISTMAS POEM (10)

The persimmon tree is heavy
with green balls.
The Mariposa plum in her white net veil
is a bride stepping shyly towards her husband
the tall fig.

Today the sea and sky merged
and a white sail glided on
like a disabled angel.
Lindy and I could see our toes
in the cool clear water.

All this, and yet I still need
the miracle of forgiveness.
Patience is the sweetest ally.
Hope and faith are rocks
piled beside the everlasting sea
as blue as my girl's eyes.

I see now I could follow joyously
with my bleating sheep
that star hope.

CHRISTMAS POEM (11)

Life is a fox slinking
beside the stone fence
its tail throbbing along
like a red feather above the stony sea.
Jack, twenty-three, longs to see
a wolf in January.
I like the blue horse, which comprises
salvia, lavender and Russian sage.
Its mane waving outside this window.
Tibetan prayer flags flutter
above the verandah opposite
my son's house and his daughters' hair
loose or in ponytails are the flags
we love. They make us jubilant
and grateful; amazed at the other miracle
this wind of hope. This morning I read
that Duchess pears are self-pollinating
but Mariposa plums are not. I saw that
faith's a pollinator too, if I can live
with doubt. It's like breathing in and out:
in is faith, out is doubt. Both comprise
the whole and bear sweet fruit.

CHRISTMAS POEM (12)

We are looking for an angel
in any form at all.
Rustle, rustle go the leaves
as the rain falls down –
the miracle of water
after it being so long dry.

Twelve ducks (ten ducklings
and their parents) play in their water bowls
under the laden plum tree –
if you want to see an ordinary miracle,
watch a duckling hatch.

Sorrow and dread began and ended this year
all the gifts of Christmas.
Yet love, trust, hope, faith and strength
are what the angel meant
and that great star it shed leading on
while we follow; some halt, some lame,
and those whose knees
or hips grind in agony
along with all our dancing children
their grace, our blessing.

'Even a live dog,' Ecclesiastes says,
'is better off than a dead lion.'
So what's a walking stick or wheelchair
when you're still alive and lucid
and outside, the moon, the stars
and somewhere among them
the angel with the news.

CHRISTMAS POEM (14)

They do not know it, but soon
they will arrive.
(What colour, or how many, no one knows.)
Like a prophet, my niece said, 'They are
our destiny.' These words made it certain.

Already, a small wooden house
with two nests of straw (bike baskets once)
sits waiting and, still, the hens are coming.
Their yard's fence-wire arrived in the night
dropped at the gate like a mystery.

So, you see, all the signs confirm
the hens are coming. It's Christmas
and the stars foretell
there'll be hens alright.

On my barrow, a discarded cupboard
of strong wood came in the gate – more nests.
Oh, the hens are welcome! Still, we wait.
Sunflowers are up and once a week
the hens will have a head of seed.
See, just say the word, have faith
and hens will come.

CHRISTMAS POEM (17)

Christmas stalks up on us
like the topknot pigeon which alighted out of the blue
this morning like a king in a turban.

In a green jug, the scent of deep cream magnolias
wafts through like prayer.
Invisible, but potent.

Silence fills the room ringing like bells –
or is it the cicadas? The garden's full
of peaches, quinces, blood oranges and plums.

Friends come to see and to drink tea.

Everything feels critical – I make a note
to take care, to pay attention, to have a fountain
of gratitude where every bird can sing.

And every friend or stranger can drink
and know that there is a miracle
sliding up towards them –

call it death, call it life, call it joy.

CHRISTMAS POEM (18)

Lightning zigzags like a broken mirror
a message across the dark slate sky.

Then, before this sentence is written,
a roll of thunder announces
that at any moment an angel may appear
holding a lightning flash, singing
the Aramaic word for peace
over and over. And what that word is
I wait to hear.

Gratitude is the sweetest gift;
paradoxically costing nothing,
like the sun. And oh, how it eases
grief with the swiftness of a coin toss.

Until today, I hadn't realised
how blessed we are that night
is full of light.

The moon and stars hang silently,
simply giving.
Christmas is coming
with its own great star
which existed before time began
in a message of glory and peace

for all, in every language
even those which have been lost
because Heaven never forgets
not even the beggar in the street
or you and me and, most radical of all,
those beautiful, old kings with their gifts.

Printed in Australia
AUHW022311280822
368236AU00009B/57

9 781743 057025